the art of
ARTHUR WATTS

COMPILED AND EDITED
BY SIMON WATTS

ARTHUR GEORGE WATTS
Artist, Sailor and Writer
1883-1935

Algrove Publishing Limited
36 Mill Street
Almonte, Ontario
Canada K0A 1A0

Telephone: (613) 256-0350
Fax: (613) 256-0360
Email: sales@algrove.com

National Library of Canada Cataloguing in Publication

Watts, Arthur, 1883-1935
    The art of Arthur Watts / [introduction] by Simon Watts.

ISBN 1-894572-83-1

    1. Watts, Arthur, 1883-1935. I. Watts, Simon II. Title.

NC1479.W38A4 2003   741.5'941   C2003-904482-3

Printed in Canada
#10803

Introduction to the Art of Arthur Watts

by Simon Watts

I was not quite six in 1935 when my father, Arthur Watts, died in a plane crash in the Swiss Alps, so my memories of him are fragmentary; mostly I remember a large friendly presence for whom I would sit, very still, while he made sketches for a drawing. However, I feel I have got to know my father through his work, not only the numerous contributions to *Punch*, the now defunct English humour magazine, but also his articles, book illustrations and an engaging account of cruising the English channel in 1913.

The humour in Arthur Watts' drawings is never spiteful or cruel. The figures he pokes fun at – the social climbers, the nouveau riche, the day trippers, the hen-pecked husbands and affected young men – are with us today, which is why so many of Arthur's drawings are just as witty and relevant as they were when first published.

Class distinctions were social fault-lines that ran right through Britain in the nineteen-twenties and thirties. Arthur's drawings often reflect this, and there are numerous cartoons where differences in accent, vocabulary, dress (especially hats), drinking habits, and even table manners are shown with acute observation and attention to detail. 'The Silver Thames' (Page 60) is only one example among many: it contrasts the sedate, middle-class picnic, complete with tablecloths and wine, with the rowdy, beer-drinking working class idea of fun.

Arthur kept some of his sharpest barbs for the 'modern' art of the period. His contorted figures in paint, plaster and stone are clever caricatures of what he saw around him. I suspect that he found most contemporary art pretentious, and pretentiousness has always been fair game for the cartoonist.

In many drawings you will find a delightful contrast between some prosaic scene at floor level and a heroic background in architecture, paintings or tapestry. The drawing on page 89, 'Courtesy–Then and Now' is a good example, or 'The Literary Lion' on page 120. Arthur often included animals in his drawings, sometimes with them making a sardonic comment on the scene. The dog in 'A Modern Christmas', page 150, and the startled horse, page 10, obviously are are giving silent expression to the artist's views.

My father often included asides in his drawings, intelligible only to family and friends, such as 'Horsnell's Hats', on page 13 and the fictitious novel, supposedly written by his daughter Margaret, advertised on the side of a bus, on page 18. 'Holly Place', the family's home in the village of Hampstead, also makes an occasional appearance.

In selecting the drawings for this book, I tried to pick those with appeal to a North American readership. I had to eliminate about a third because the humour was dated, the reference too obscure or the caption unwieldy. I changed very few of the original captions, just adding a note of explanation where necessary. Some details in these drawings might be considered offensive by today's standards, but bear in mind the era in which they were produced. Tracking down all the drawings, some 70 or 80 years old, and making acceptable copies has involved a great deal of research. I am especially grateful to the staff of the *Punch* Library and Archive in London as well as the San Francisco Library's Special Collections Department. My family and friends have also encouraged this project by making original work available for scanning.

This book is dedicated to Arthur Watts' grandchildren and great grandchildren.

Simon Watts, San Francisco, 2003

For more on Arthur Watts' work, including railway posters and articles in Yachting Monthly, *see the website at* www.arthurwatts.com.

Arthur Watts Remembered

by Marjorie Watts*

Arthur Watts was born in 1883, his father being a surgeon-major in the Indian Medical Service. He had achieved this position by hard work and dogged determination, his own father being a chemist in Peckham, and he expected his sons to enter professions. The older brother became a doctor, but Arthur, who ruined all his school exercise books with funny drawings in the margins, only wanted to draw, and sat at the bottom of the class on the Engineering side at Dulwich School for two years, until at 16 he was allowed to go to the Goldsmith's Institute.

His father then died, and his mother, who had a lovely voice and had herself wanted to be a singer, but had not been allowed to train, did all she could for him. In 1900, aged 17, he went to the Slade Art School for two years, and from there to the Free Art Schools in Antwerp, then to Paris and then back to the Slade for a short time under the redoubtable Professor Tonks.

In 1904, aged 21, Arthur began to make a modest living by drawing for such papers as *The Tatler*, *The Bystander*, *Pearson's*, and *London Opinion*, and in 1912 made his first contribution to *Punch*. For some years he had been interested in boats and sailing, and in 1910, whilst intending to buy a Great Dane dog through the Exchange and Mart, he saw a sailing boat advertised and bought her instead, with a centre board, mainsail and jib. Arthur rapidly became a skilled small boat sailor and began to write illustrated articles for *The Yachting Monthly*. One called 'From London to Lowestoft in an Open Boat' was published in 1911, and another, 'A Three-Legged Cruise', in August, 1913. He now had a bigger boat, 'a comparatively fragile affair, O.A. length 26 ft, and beam 6 ft 6 ins, with a centre board – 3 tons'. With two friends in a second boat – 'a respectable Itchen Ferry type of 4 tons' – and with a well-read copy of Erskine Childers' *Riddle of the Sands* in his pocket, Arthur and his two friends set off in the two boats in June 1913 for a three-week cruise along the Dutch and Belgian coasts. They sailed into a dozen or so harbours, including Dunkirk, Blanckenburg, Veere, the Tholen Creek, Middleburg, Zerixsee, and Ostend and Zeebrugge, together with a host of canals and waterways. A detailed description of this voyage, with drawings of all the harbours they visited, was published in *The Yachting Monthly* in August 1913.

And in August 1914, the First World War began.

Meanwhile in 1911 Arthur had rented No. 1, Holly Place, Hampstead, where the landlords, the Catholic Church, built up the two attics to make a studio which overlooked London and enabled their tenant to practice his 'birds-eye' style of drawing.

In the autumn of 1914, on calling at the Admiralty to offer his services, he was welcomed without surprise. His *Yachting Monthly* articles, detailing the Dutch and Belgian harbours, had not passed unnoticed. He joined the R.N.V.R. and served throughout the war in Coastal Motor Boats and Motor Launches in the Dover Patrol. He led a smoke-screen flotilla at the attacks on Zeebrugge on April 23rd and at Ostend on May 10th, 1918. He was awarded the D.S.O. and mentioned in Despatches. The citation read:

> *Lieut.-Cdr. Arthur G. Watts, R.N.V.R.*
> *This officer was in command of M.L. 239 and leader of a smoke-screen unit with skill*
> *and judgment in a very exposed position, and it was largely due to him that the screen*
> *was so extremely successful in his section.*

The attacking force had to wait 3 weeks, in absolute secrecy, for the right wind and tide to coincide, and there were two false starts when they had to turn back owing to a change of wind. Arthur said later that he was absolutely terrified all that time – inside himself – and was amazed that no one seemed to notice this.

One of the most famous ships in the Zeebrugge attack was the old cruiser, *H.M.S. Vindictive*, whose job was to land troops on the Mole, whilst screened by the smoke from the motor launches. Although terribly battered, the old Vindictive (built in 1898) did her job and managed to return to Dover under her own power. For a fascinating account of this whole battle, I recommend *The Zeebrugge Raid* by Philip Warner, published by William Kimber.

After his experiences in both raids, Arthur was badly shell-shocked, and it was not until 1921 that his work began to appear again in *Punch* – they published eight of his drawings during 1922, after which his reputation grew until it reached its peak in 1935.

Apart from *Punch*, *The Radio Times* formed a focal point in Arthur's working life, since he did four small drawings for the pages 'Both Sides of the Microphone' every week for seven years from 1928 to 1935, never missing one issue. He also illustrated E.M. Delafield's *Diary of a Provincial Lady* and drew a number of posters for London Transport and the old London, Midland and Scottish Railway. Unfortunately, all the originals of the L.M.S. drawings vanished during the nationalization period. Luckily, I still own a few copies of some of those posters, which are in the Exhibition**. As for Arthur's personal life, I will leave his contemporaries to speak for him, in the obituary notices published after his death by *Punch* and *The Radio Times*.

In Memoriam - Punch July 31, 1935

It was with very deep regret that we learned of the tragic death in an aeroplane disaster of July 20th of Arthur Watts, whose delightful full-page drawings are so well known to Punch *readers. Mr. Watts, who was born in 1883, began his long association with* Punch *some years before the Great War, in which he served with much distinction, reaching the rank of Commander in the R.N.V.R. and gaining the D.S.O. at the Zeebrugge Raid on April 23rd, 1918. Two examples of the quiet humour and careful craftsmanship, which always distinguished his work, are included in this issue. His loss, both as a friend and as an artist, will be most keenly felt.*

Arthur Watts - Radio Times August 2, 1936

For the first time in more than seven years, these pages appear without their illustrations by Arthur Watts. His tragic death in an air crash, on his way home from Italy, was announced over the microphone on the evening of Saturday, July 20. At that date, last week's issue of The Radio Times *was already in the Press, containing the last batch of drawings that he posted from Italy. The paragraphs for this week's issue were already awaiting his return.*

We need not here stress his pre-eminence as a humorous artist. Our readers know his quality well enough, though it is possible that nobody who has not had experience of such work can realize quite what an achievement it was to keep up the standard of those four drawings a week all year round; drawings done to order, done often in a hurry, and confined to a shape that would tax the ingenuity of the most resourceful. Occasionally even Watts protested; we remember the occasion when he drew a euphonium-player lying down . . .

Personally, he seemed far less like the popular idea of a humorous artist than like the Commander R.N.V.R. that he also was. A big, quiet man, with ruddy, weather-beaten face, dressed almost invariably in a blue jacket and well-worn grey flannel trousers; smoking a pipe bound with tarred twine; driving a big, roomy, powerful old car; spending his summers in Cornwall, and every winter taking a skiing holiday. . .

We shall remember him in his studio at Hampstead, with a view half across London, where he worked at the delicate little drawings with which he gave so much pleasure – which were, incidentally, the last sort of work that anybody who knew him only casually would have expected him to do.

None of our readers can fail to realize what a gap his death will leave upon these pages. It is not for us to enlarge on the loss that will be felt elsewhere.

Marjorie Watts was Arthur Watts' wife. Marjorie Watts' mother, Amy Dawson Scott, was a prolific writer (sometimes under the pen-name Sappho) and the founder of PEN, the organization of poets, editors and novelists. Marjorie Watts wrote the published biography of her mother, Mrs. Sappho: The Life of C. A. Dawson Scott, Mother of International PEN.

**Arthur Watts Remembered, *December 9 to February 28, 1982. An exhibition of* Punch *cartoons, illustrations, posters, sketches and drawings. Burgh House, New End Square, Hampstead, London NW3 1LT.*

Table of Contents

Chapter 3

Chapter 1

Black and White Work
of Arthur Watts

arthur watts

Art, Artists and Performers

"Didn't the artist finish them things, Albert?"
"O' course they did, stupid. It's dustin's done that."

Ultra-modern portrait painter to restive sitter: "My dear Madam, how can you
expect me to obtain a good portrait of you unless you sit still?"

If every actor had his rights.
(When actors command the same attention off-stage as on-stage)

The World's Worst Seller

"I do wish we'd gone to the pictures, Emma".

The owner: "But it ***does*** give you a feeling of movement?"
The other: "Yes, horribly."

"What do they do with the old ones, Daddy?"

A pavement artist holds a private view of some new works.
(A backyard gallery reception, complete with refreshments, discerning patrons–and nosy neighbours.)

"Didn't I tell yer not to let the pore old feller see it, George?"

"If I could only get a little more *breadth* into it."

arthur watts

Autos, Cars, Traffic and Mishaps

The Oasis
(*An amazing range of period vehicles. Arthur often labeled passing buses and vans with the
names of family and friends. Jimmy Horsnell was a theatre critic, the Farjeons were close neighbours.*)

arthur watts

The man who had a little wallpaper left over.

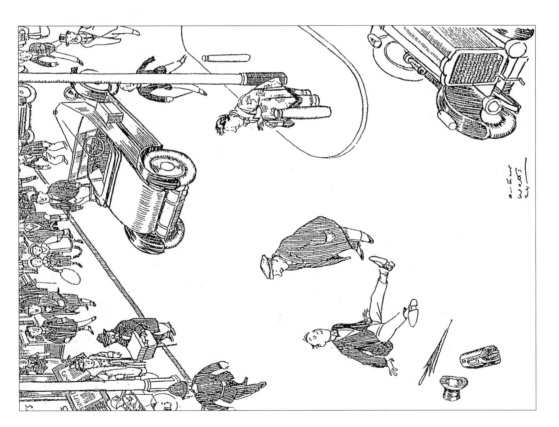

Enthusiastic motorist: "By Jove, Sir, the springing of that little car of mine's a marvel! Do you know, until I heard people shouting, I'd no idea I'd run over you."

What it feels like when you make a really bad gear change.
*(An excruciating sound often heard before synchromesh,
an invention that took the guesswork out of gear-changing.)*

Force of habit.
Retired plumber: "Well, stand by, Emma, while I go back for me tools."
(Plumbers had a reputation for never having the right tools for a job.)

Mistress (to the cause of all the trouble): "Did the nasty car try to run over mother's precious, then?"

Bus driver (to small car cutting in): "And who might you think you was? The Flying Squad?"
(The 'Flying Squad', formed in 1918, was Scotland Yard's version of a Rapid
Deployment Force. Margaret Watts [on bus] was the artist's daughter, my
half sister, and Jimmy Horsnell was the most unlikely man to tangle with a lion.)

"Oh, Henry. Don't you just *love* these great open spaces."

19

"No wonder she seized up, Ethel. There's no water in the radiator."
(*The notice board reads:* Ideal Camping Sites)

Misleading terms: 'The Level Crossing.'
(This crossing still exists, just outside Bodmin, in North Cornwall, although there are no more trains.)

Police officer: "I said draw in to the kerb. You've got an inefficient silencer on your machine."
Motorcyclist: "Sorry, old fellow. That infernal machine's making such a noise I can't hear a word you're saying."

(Silencer = Muffler. Addressing the police as 'old fellow' might not go
down too well today. The side of the van reads: 'Jimmy and Arthur'.)

"Nothing serious, dear. Got run over by a horse."
(A cart horse could easily have out-weighed the car, and not been much inferior in power.)

The Lorry Driver: "And tell me–do you find you like London."
(Lorry=Truck. A man's station in life could be judged by his hat.
Bumpus' was a well-known bookseller.)

"Why can't you remember to turn the wireless off when you leave the car, Henry?"
(There is still a pub called 'Dog and Duck' at Lambeth Green.)

Why not a *School for Pedestrians*?

arthur watts

Big Game Hunting, Exploring, Sports and Animals

Joy-Riding in the Alps
Impression of a nervous gentleman being overtaken, while lugeing, by a bobsleigh.

"Dear Henry. Splendid skiing here. Lost the rest of the party yesterday
and came down through the woods without taking a single toss."
(The wooden skis of the period were simply enormous—seven or even eight feet long.)

Following the popular fashion in 'atmospheric' dressing, Colonel Blood arranges
local colour for his talk on Big Game Hunting in Mumbo Jumbah.

"Dammit! Where's the brute got to?"

"No, there aren't any more cartridges, dear. Would this tin of rat-poison be any good?"

arthur watts

Boats and Boating Mishaps, Yachts and Flying

Cockney Oarsman (to yachtsman who is tacking in a sailing dinghy): "Ere! Why
can't yer sail straight instead o' zig-zagging all over the river like that?"
*(This, in 1912, is the first of my father's many contributions to Punch.
The upper crust sailor, with yachting cap, blazer and tie, versus the
working class oarsman, bowler hat, suspenders and Cockney diction.)*

Bridge fiend: "Drat it! It's clearing up and I suppose
we shall have to go out in that confounded boat."

"A diver's work must be very dangerous."
"Yes, Mum, 'specially if they go down wiv a cold."
"A cold?"
"Yes, Mum, the pore fellows sneeze and bust their dresses."
(Longshoremen were always ready to spin unlikely yarns to unsuspecting tourists.)

The boatman who observed to an admiral that it was a fine day for a sail.

Chatty visitor to officer of the watch: "And which do
you prefer, young man—steamships or sail boats?"

"You might have upset the beastly thing a bit further out, George.
I'd rather be drowned than look a perfect fool."

Jones gets tired of flying with a friend in the rain.

Modern Sightseeing
"Salisbury Cathedral! The Highest Spire in England!"

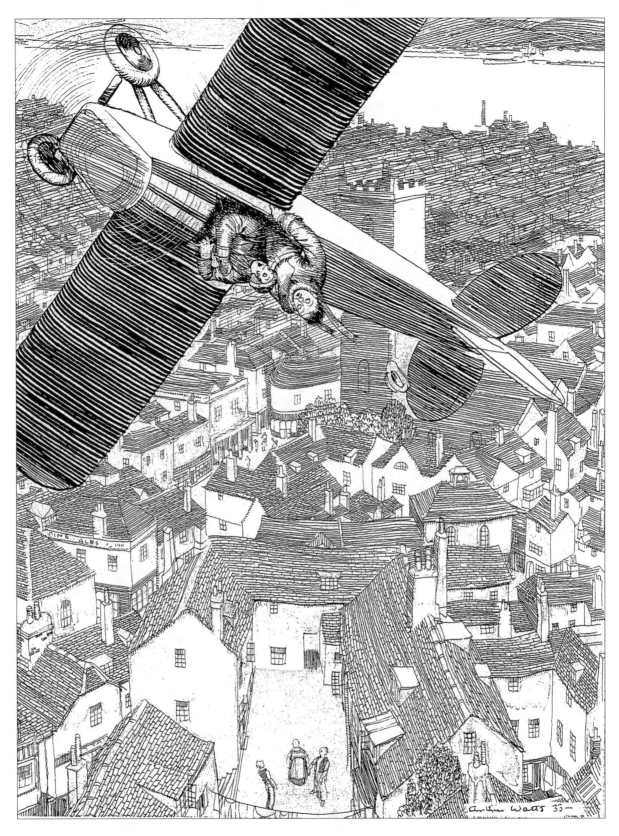

"Mind where you're going, Ethel."
"I can't help it, John. There's a mouse in the cockpit."

42

arthur watts

Buildings Old and New

"I can't see the use of wastin' a lot of money patching up them old houses, Perce.
They can't get 'em to look like new ones when they've done it."

"I do wish you hadn't lent Henry that book on archaeology, Mr. Boffin."

Progress
(This nostalgic scene depicts the impending demolition of a gracious old mansion to make room for the masses of cheap housing run up between the two world wars. The phrases 'ribbon development' and 'jerry-building' were coined about this time.)

arthur watts

Christmas and All That

Seasonable Conversation
"What always fascinates me, of course, is the underlying sadness of things."

"Noticed Lord and Lady B. this morning choosing
Christmas presents in a famous West-End store."
(It was customary to give the servants gifts on Boxing Day, the day after Christmas.)

Temptation; or the man who remembers too late that
he had *forgotten* to buy his wife a Christmas present.

"I'm afraid we've had to cut down on the Christmas
decorations this year, Smithers. Do the best you can with this."
(*Smithers is the generic butler expected to deal tactfully with any eventuality.*)

"And the next time I hear you whistling 'Hark, the
Herald Angels Sing', I'll wring your little neck."
(The year that Edward VIII gave up the throne to marry an American divorcée, the street
urchins were singing: 'Hark, the herald angels sing, Mrs. Simpson's pinched our King'.)

52

"Excuse me, M'Lady, the contractors have called to fix the mistletoe."

arthur watts

Drinking, Night Clubs and the Law

The Suspect
Study of a detective mingling with the crowd at a night-club.

"I tell you they are police officers–they're drinking champagne."
*(Although England never experienced prohibition, drinking
hours were regulated and the laws strictly enforced.)*

Short-sighted water-diviner, divining temperance friend in crowded restaurant.

"Isn't there **anywhere** here we can get a drink?"
(*Licensing laws prohibited public houses from opening before 6 p.m. However,
if you were a 'bone fide' traveler, you could be served. A thirsty group of locals
often hired a bus to take them to the pub in the next village—and vice versa.*)

Haunts of Romance Series

These drawings are from the 'Haunts of Romance' series.
The theme, how the objects of mass tourism become
diminished and degraded, is as relevant now as
it was in the 1920s when these were drawn.

Haunts of Romance: The Silver Thames.
(Easy to distinguish the middle classes, with their table cloths, tea cups and wine bottles, from the rowdies tossing litter, drinking beer, playing concertinas and generally enjoying themselves.)

Haunts of Romance: The State Apartments.

Haunts of Romance: The Leafy Lane.
(These open sightseeing buses, called 'char-a-bancs', were a menace in narrow country lanes.)

Haunts of Romance: The Smuggler's Cave.

Haunts of Romance: The Waterfall.

Haunts of Romance: The Lonely Lake.

Haunts of Romance: The Hall of the Kings.

arthur watts

Summer Holidays and Camping

"Seems silly now to have gone to the Lake District for our holiday, doesn't it, George?"

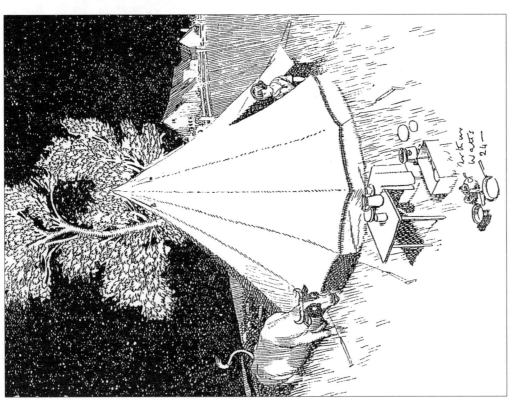

Fond wife (whose husband has gone to the farm for supplies):
"The opening's on the other side, darling."
(Arthur's mother-in-law, Mrs. Dawson Scott, lived in what was called a 'bell tent' like this one, much of the Cornish summer. I suspect that this harmless eccentricity was the inspiration for this drawing.)

Arrival of the fat customer. Stampede in the donkey market.
*(At this time people didn't hide behind euphemisms when it came
to such words as fat, dwarf, blind, stupid, crippled or mad.)*

"Dash it, Flo! I think it was Biarritz the Robinsons said
was so gay in the winter and not Ostend at all."
*(Ostend is a cold, wind-swept seaside town in Belgium.
Biarritz is a wealthy resort 500 miles to the south.)*

Mr. Jones, the Covent Garden porter, sets out on his annual holiday.
*(Porters in Covent Garden, London's wholesale vegetable market,
routinely carried a stack of laden baskets on their heads.)*

Bank holiday and the law.
"Persons depositing paper, litter or rubbish of any sort on this open space will be prosecuted."

"Well, darling, we couldn't have chosen a lovelier country than Switzerland for a walking tour."
"No dear—except Holland."

The man who couldn't get away this year.
('Getting Away' from the factory chimneys
belching smoke in the background.)

"Do you remember that awful time, Henry,
when all the pipes burst?"

Wife of professional strong man: "Why can't you give over
that silly 'abit of chucking stones into the sea, Bert?"

"Of course, if I lived here, I'd have the sweetest little rock garden."

"No, it's odd; *I* always feel I want to throw somebody *else* off the cliff."

"I'm quite prepared to rescue you, sir, but would you kindly not keep on saying 'Oi' at me?"
*(This is Mother Ivy's beach, near Trevose Head, in Cornwall. I remember
it being extremely steep—you were out of your depth in only a few steps,
so the swimmer's predicament is not only possible but likely.)*

"I'm beginning to wish we'd bought the car first, Ethel."

arthur watts

London Underground (Tube)

Tout Passé
Time and the escalator wait for no man.

What happened to the man who <u>would</u> sit on the stairs.
*(Moving stairs (escalators) were still an innovation in 1923
and not as foolproof as we like to think they are today.)*

The Underground's new interpreters meet their Bannockburn.
(*'Bannockburn' was a famous battle in 1314 when the Scots soundly defeated
an English army. The officials are clearly baffled by the Scot's brogue,
thickened, no doubt, by the contents of the bottle in his pocket.*)

arthur watts

Love, Courtship, Marriage and Children

"Will beautiful lady in black hat, to whom admirer offered seat in Hampstead Tube, meet him under clock at Charing Cross Station, Friday, 6:30 p.m.?"

The Course of True Love

The Connoisseurs
(An 'objet d'art' can take many forms.)

Sympathy

Courtesy–Then and Now
(An alternative title is pencilled on the back of the original drawing:
'Lovers, Ancient and Modern'.)

"Oh, you naughty boy to smack your little brother's face!"
"Well, it ain't any use smackin' 'im anywhere else—it don't 'urt 'im."

Voice: "Is Mrs. Jones in?" *Jones:* "No, she's away for the weekend."
Voice: "Who's minding the baby?" *Jones:* "I do–awfully."
(The wall hangings add an ironic comment to the scene below–and so does the inevitable dog.)

If everyone thought Miss Jones as lovely as Mr. Smith does.

Infatuation
(*The modern traveler can have no idea of the sheer volume of smoke,
steam and noise that accompanied every departure from a mainline station.*)

The guard who'd just got engaged himself.

"There's no one like you anywhere in the world, Gertrude."
(My mother, Marjorie, was the model for this masterly drawing.)

Why not brighter civil weddings?

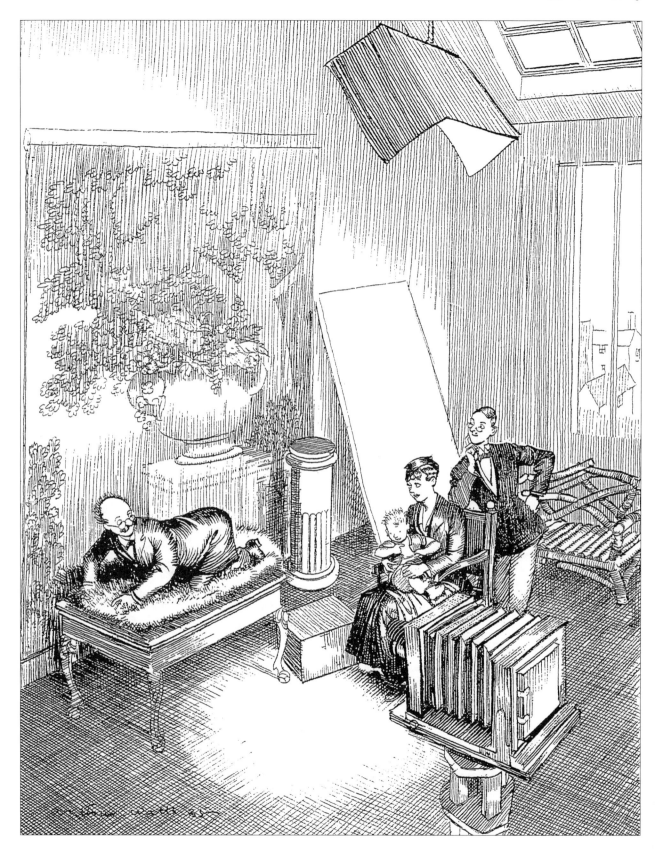

"There! If we could only get the little fellow looking like this."

arthur watts

Men's Clubs, Night Clubs, Parties and Conservatism

General Boome sends out for a paper to find that, owing
to labour troubles, only the 'Daily Worker' is available.
(The Daily Worker was the Communist Party newspaper and a red rag to the conservatives of the day.)

The unconventional club call! The wife who didn't believe the hall porter.
(When a man went to his club, he expected to be secure from even the threat of female intrusion.)

A number of distinguished people assembled at
Lady X's to meet the Boravian Chargé d'Affaires.

101

UNLIKELY EVENTS
The Times starts a comic strip.

"Sorry, old chap. Can't get round tonight. Got some people here."

arthur watts

Rural, Domestic and Suburban Life

Balloonist (drifting at the mercy of the gale): "Hi! Are
we anywhere near Cambridge?"
Rustic: "No. You want to turn sharp to the right."
(A typical balloon of the period with wicker basket, sand bags for ballast and a grapnel.)

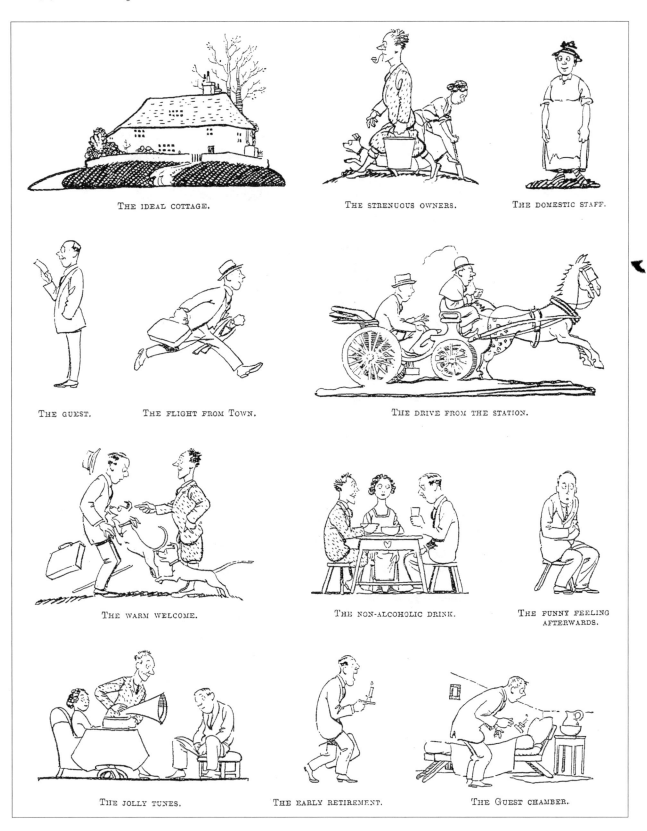

THE IDEAL COTTAGE.   THE STRENUOUS OWNERS.   THE DOMESTIC STAFF.

THE GUEST.   THE FLIGHT FROM TOWN.   THE DRIVE FROM THE STATION.

THE WARM WELCOME.   THE NON-ALCOHOLIC DRINK.   THE FUNNY FEELING AFTERWARDS.

THE JOLLY TUNES.   THE EARLY RETIREMENT.   THE GUEST CHAMBER.

A weekend at an ideal cottage (part one).
(This was shortly before the author Stella Gibbons came out with her book, 'Cold Comfort Farm', a hilarious parody of country living.)

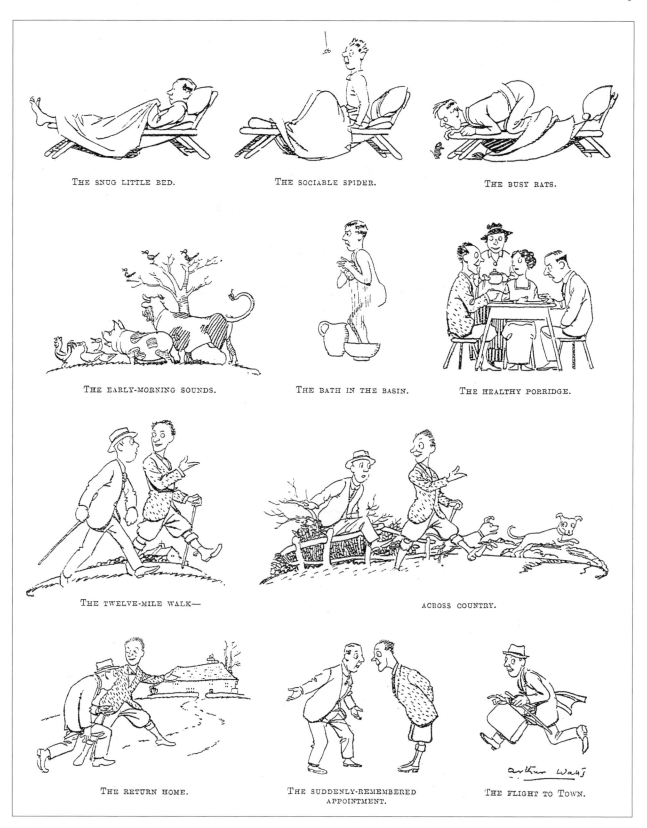

A weekend at an ideal cottage (part two).

GLIMPSE OF THE UNDERWORLD
Maid (in a hoarse whisper): "Excuse me, Mum, cook sez
she's very sorry but she's trod on the pudding."

Farmer: "How did ye come by that black eye, Jarge?"
Jarge: "Ole cow had a way o' flickin' me face wit' her tail, so
I tied a brick onto it."

Our vicar's wife buys a new hat.

The Laurels joins the 'Back to the Land' movement.

Local people viewing the newly decorated village hall with frescoes depicting
'Rural Life' painted by Sir Timothy Weazel's daughter, Miss Winifred Weazel.
(Arthur combined two local Cornish names, calling the village 'Little Issey.'
No doubt Sir Timothy is presiding, with the Vicar alongside. A delicious contrast
between the heroic figures on the walls and the bemused and amused spectators.)

The Nightingale

Unfortunate incident during our production of *A Midsummer's Night's Dream* at Little Oozeley.

"Oh, Mr. Pendlebury, could you catch our kitten for us?"

"It looks a *little* better already, darling!"

arthur watts

Society, Social Climbing, Pretension and Britishness

Disgraced; or, the writing on the van.
(Buying on the installment plan, or hire purchase, was often a source of embarrassment.
Perhaps just part of a general British reticence about sex and money matters.)

"And this room would make a nice cozy little den for you, Wilfred."
(The pretentiousness of the nouveau riche was always good for a laugh. A tinge of envy, perhaps?)

The man who ordered shrimps at a *Thé Dansant*.
*(One was supposed to drink tea at a 'thé dansant', and not order working class food
like shrimps or sardines on toast. Nor did one powder one's nose at the tea table.)*

The Literary Lion
(These rather overstuffed ladies have captured a real, live author. My grandmother, Arthur's mother-in-law, Amy Dawson Scott, was not only a novelist herself, but founder of P.E.N., still an influential world-wide organization of writers. She frequently entertained visiting writers.)

Ambitious hostess: "My dear, we've arrived. There were
no fewer than fourteen gate-crashers here tonight."

121

"Ruined, Albert? And shall we have to leave our little nest?"

Prospective tenant: "Eh, lass. Back yard's champion!"
(Wealthy industrialists with Midlands vocabulary and accents were often figures of fun.)

arthur watts

Miscellaneous

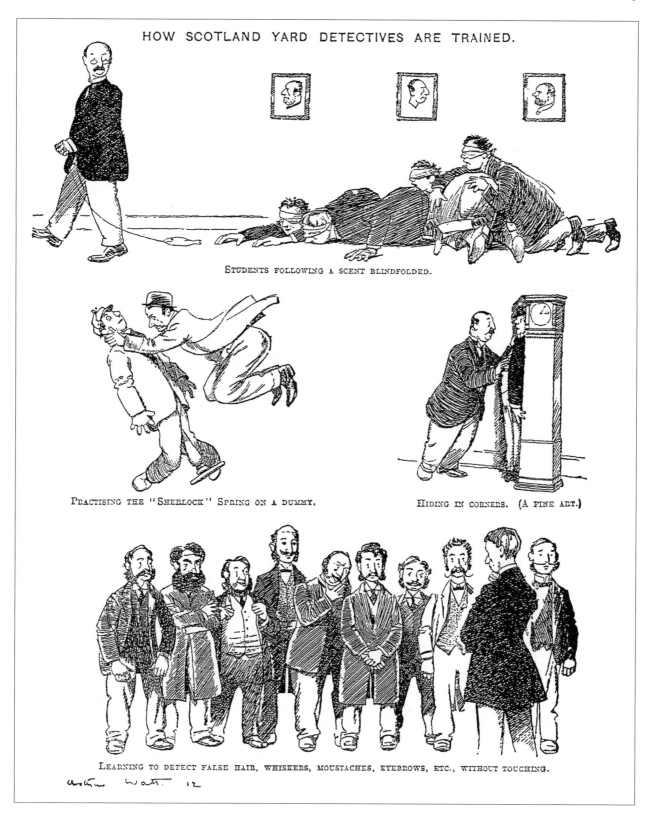

How Scotland Yard detectives are trained.
Students following a scent blindfolded; Practicing the *Sherlock Spring* on a dummy;
Hiding in Corners (A Fine Art); Learning to detect false hair, mustaches,
eyebrows, etc., without actually touching.

THE ROSARY.

THE SOLDIERS' CHORUS.

DOWN DIXIE.

By the bandstand…a responsive audience.
The Rosary, The Soldier's Chorus, Down Dixie…

A busy day at Los Angeles, the capital of filmland.
(Probably a not-too-exaggerated view of what middle-class England thought went on in Hollywood.)

The passenger (in the floating-palace liner): "Excuse me, steward, but could you tell me the way to the sea?"

"I say, waiter, this food's shocking. Who've you got in the kitchen?"
"The police, sir."
(An alternative to this caption reads:
"I say, waiter, this food's shocking. Call the manager"
"He won't eat it either, sir.")

Proprietor of antique shop in 2050: Quaint old piece that. Petrol pump
from the early motoring days. Would make quite a charming hall lamp.

Absent-minded salesman: "Yes, sir. A unique piece–we sell a lot of them."

"Yes, Rupert, that's an aspidistra. Mother was feeling a little homesick."
*(A plant typifying lower class taste. 'Keep the Aspidistra Flying'
was one of George Orwell's lesser known writings.)*

"If you're so fond of the goldfish, Ruby, why don't
you come down and help me look for them?"

The false note.
(Everything in such good taste—except the bottle of beer.)

SHY GAME
or, the two pence taker who wouldn't give up.
(*Chairs cost two pence per hour–park benches were free.*)

The Dowser at Work
"No, sir, I am unable to detect a trace of water."

"Smithers speaking, sir. The kitchen boiler is giving trouble."
*(Combining British Understatement with a Stiff Upper Lip. One can hear the
voice at the other end of the telephone saying, "Jolly good, Smithers, carry on.")*

Mrs. Jones (faintly): "John, we can't go on like this."

Chapter 2

Colour Work
of Arthur Watts

The good joke.

"Just run 'ome an' fetch me my small 'ammer, Albert."

Fisherman (in extremely sophisticated Cornish town):
"Ah, following in the footsteps of Van Gogh, sir!"
(This must have been Padstow, on the north coast of Cornwall, England.
If anything, the town has become even more 'arty' since this 1929 drawing.)

Our market town tries out the rotary system.
(*According to Bill Bryson (author of* Mother Tongue) 'Goat and Compasses'
is a corruption of 'God Encompasseth Us.')

arthur watts

View of a public park in Scotland.
(In my view, the Scots have an undeserved reputation for stinginess;
chairs rented for two pence an hour while benches were free.)

Passer-by (to extremely eccentric-looking artist): "Might I ask, sir, why you choose the height of summer for depicting this landscape in the depth of winter?"
Eccentric artist: "Certainly; it's so much warmer."

Homesickness or the Call of the Jungle
*(Organ grinders with their red-jacketed monkeys, along with
Punch and Judy shows, are on the fringes of my memory.)*

The wireless: "Miss Lucille Wordsworth will now give us
her talk on winter sports and what to wear."

arthur watts

The guide: "Take it easy, sir, and keep your strength for the difficult part."
(When an Englishman loses his hat you know he's really in trouble.)

The bargee: "And where did you come from, baby dear?"
(Bargees had a reputation for foul language, independence and scorn for 'gentlemen' yachtsmen.)

arthur watts

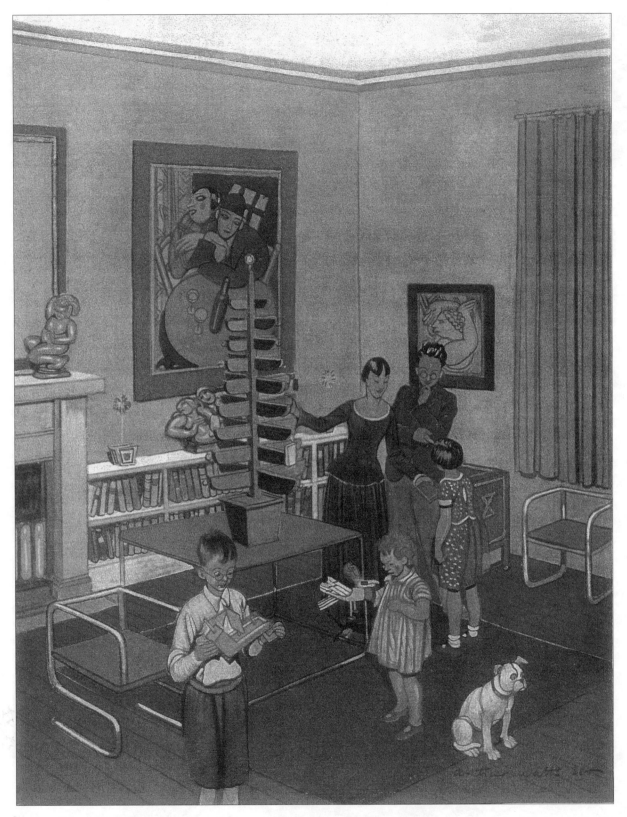

A Modern Christmas
"And there's a nice little book on Picasso for you, Laura."
(I especially like the caricature of the famous Bauhaus tubular steel furniture—drawn
exactly right but backwards. As usual, the dog gives expression to the artist's feelings.)

Painful predicament of explorer who, finding it essential to his morale
to dress for dinner every evening, loses his only collar-stud.

Our ex-sergeant-major gets the job of town crier.
(Sergeant-Majors were known for the strength of their lungs and general assertiveness.)

The Continuous Performance
*(The bull is trying to decide whether to charge the booth or
enjoy the performance. Punch and Judy in a tight spot.)*

Hall porter: "Seems like the good old times, Sir Henry, to see a member with the gout again."
(A tactless remark–given that gout is a painful circulatory disorder.)

The Christmas Spirit
(The attention to detail in this dizzying view is characteristic: the smoke from the steamer and the set of the sails in the two vessels are all consistent with the wind direction as indicated by the weather vane.)

155

"Fat lot all these people see of the country, driving about in closed cars."

The Outsider
('Outsiders' were huntsmen who joined in a hunt although they
were not members of the local meet—but not usually on wheels!)

"Oh, do stop grumbling, Arthur. You wanted an
old-fashioned Christmas and now you've got one."

158

Ignominy.
*(Snow-ploughing, sitting on his poles to brake, burdened
by a knapsack...this chap is definitely not cool.)*

"Flown the Atlantic, have ye? Then supposin' you catch my cows and tell them about it!"

"No Sir. This is 'Hill Rise'. 'Hill Crest' is over there."

Chapter 3

Articles by Arthur Watts
for "The Artist" Magazine

Arthur Watts was killed when he was 52 in a civil flying crash in July, 1935.
In May of that year he wrote the last of six articles on 'Black and White Drawing –
Solving Some of Its Problems', which were published in *The Artist*. Since what
he wrote represented exactly what he believed, in his maturity and at the peak
of his career, it seemed appropriate to re-print these articles, which may be of
interest to artists and students in his field 47 years later.

Marjorie Watts
January, 1982

Black and White Drawing–
Solving Some of Its Problems

By Arthur Watts

Part 1. December, 1934

In this series of articles, which the Editor had asked me to write for *THE ARTIST*, I propose to deal with black and white drawing and its difficulties from the point of view of the student.

I propose to look back on my own career – well, career seems rather a grandiloquent word, but I cannot think of any better – and soliloquize on the many mistakes that I know only too clearly I have made, and point out the errors that I would avoid if I could have my time over again. Then, after a few observations on the general training of students, I think we may go on to the questions of good and bad style, of how black and white drawings are made, and the best methods by which good reproductions can be obtained. You shall see a finished *Punch* drawing, with the pencil studies for it, and I think we might have a talk on that delightful medium, scraper board.

To start with, if I were in the happy position of being a student again I should approach drawing from the life very differently.

From the sketch book of Arthur Watts.

From the sketch book of Arthur Watts.

Instead of drawing the figure divorced from its background, I would always attempt to get it into the proper relation with the wall, curtain, or whatever was behind it. Because, to fit your figures into the scene to which they belong, especially when you are using models, is always one of the chief difficulties in composing a drawing. And instead of doing a composition for the school sketch club 'out of my head', I would carry it further by using models. I do not mean professional models – they are too expensive for most students – I mean using any fellow student or relative who could be cajoled into sitting.

As I remember it, learning to use models was a heart-rending business. I would have an idea for a figure composition; make a composition with vague figures all decoratively inclined to one another; and the result, to myself at least, was most successful. But when I came to trying to work the thing out from models! All the life went; all the decorative swing of the thing went; nothing was left but some wooden, meaningless figures.

Like a fool, I often produced, or tried to produce, finished drawings without models. Now in art you cannot lay down any laws, but it is safe to say that in figure work the model is indispensable. I do not say that good work has not been done without them – but I do say that for ninety-nine people out of a

hundred they are essential. So, unless you are quite certain that you are a genius, make up your mind to use a model wherever possible.

Learn earlier what it took me so many years to learn: that your study is only made as a guide, that many – most – of its details are irrelevant, and that your only need is to correct your memory and observation. If, for instance you are drawing a man in modern dress, you will find that, however well his clothes fit, there are all sorts of accidental folds that do not at all suggest the figure underneath; that have no real significance, that are, as I say, irrelevant. Put them in your study if you like; make it as careful as you can; but in your finished drawing, for which the study was made, eliminate the inessentials.

Speaking of memory and observation, how much I wish that I had trained mine more. How I wish I had employed that excellent method of looking at an object, going into another room to draw it, returning to refresh

From the sketch book of Arthur Watts.

my memory, and so on, until that drawing was completed without it and the object ever having met, as it were. What a training for an artist interested primarily in character, who sees for a minute a face which, if he cannot draw from memory, he will never draw at all!

From the sketch book of Arthur Watts.

I believe I am right in saying that, ages before such a thing as photography was even guessed at, this was the method by which Chinese artists were taught and, for all I know to the contrary, still is. So developed did their powers of observation and memory become by this training that by shutting their eyes, opening them for the fraction of a second, and shutting them again, they could keep in their minds the visual image of what they saw long enough to be able to transfer that visual image to paper. It was in this manner that they were enabled to draw insects and birds in flight, and it is an indubitable fact that, when the camera was invented and 'instantaneous' pictures were produced, it was proved by comparison that these artists' memorisations were perfectly accurate.

I tried that method myself, but, having no stern master to goad me on and, alas that I should have to say it, being constitutionally lazy, dropped it; for it is the most exhausting form of study that I know. Yes, thinking the matter over, I believe I would put this aspect of a student's training before life drawing; before every other form of study.

I know it is often said that anyone who can draw the nude can draw anything, and, as long as that person is drawing what he sees in front of him, I agree. But the whole difficulty of my profession, the profession of a man whose business is to record the life going on around him, is that he must be continually representing what he cannot see, or sees only in details at different times and under different circumstances.

From the sketch book of Arthur Watts.

165

From the sketch book of Arthur Watts.

How many, how pathetically many, students can turn out a really able drawing 'from the life'; but how few can draw and make convincing a crowd of people in a street, or a dog running.

Yes, that is what it comes to. If you are going to be one of those artists who confine themselves to the expression of form, of form displayed before them, comparatively motionless, then stick to your life class. But if you want to draw the human scene, or if you want to express subjects almost *en fugitif*, as elusive as the birds in flight that the old Chinese artists drew so well, then let the nude take second place, and observation and memorisation first.

Now what I have just said may seem at variance with what I said a little while ago about the importance of using models. It is not really. You will remember that I said the model should be used as a guide, a check to your memory and observation. Supposing you have seen a character that you want to express – well, blend the two together. Rough your figure out; get as far as you possibly can from memory; and then from a model get such details as will give the drawing a roundness, a solidity, that will probably be lacking without his or her help.

From the sketch book of Arthur Watts.

Let us say you are drawing a French *gendarme* from memory. You remember with tolerable accuracy the kind of face he had; how his mustache grew; and you remember too – this, alas, is where my badly trained memory lets me down – the details of his cloak and buttons. Still, a study of a figure approximating to his figure, in ordinary coat and trousers, standing in the pose you want your gendarme to stand in, will help you; it will serve as a framework on which to hang your accessories. Obviously, if you could get a real gendarme to sit for you, that would be better still. I only say that this framework, with the drawing you will get of the hands, the shadows on the features, the folds, the broad folds of the clothes, will help you.

"Gendarme" from the drawings of Arthur Watts.

As to learning figure composition, that is a thing I am a little doubtful about. Composition is simply another word for design, and your eye, if you are by nature an artist, should tell you without any resort to rules whether a design is good or bad. It is a debatable point, I know, but in my opinion too close a study of the theory of design tends to give a student a rather conventional habit of composition.

If I take this subject rather lightly, it is because I know that if I have any talent at all, which in my gloomier moments I am inclined to doubt, it is for design, and as far as I remember I never had a lesson in this subject. But if you are less fortunate, and are better draftsman than designer, I would recommend

From the sketch books of Arthur Watts.

frequent excursions to the British and the Victoria and Albert museums. The latter is my favorite, I admit; it has not that rather dreary acreage of 'specimens', and is altogether a much more human institution. Moreover there is, especially for penniless students, a superb library where, for nothing, you may see and read all the finest works on art that have ever been produced. For those who live in the provinces the matter is more difficult, I know; nonetheless, even if you are reduced to your local library, there are many books to be found that will stimulate you to a better appreciation of design.

Detail sketch by Arthur Watts.

But to go back to the Victoria and Albert museum, what a treasure house that place is! Hall after hall, gallery after gallery, of everything that is lovely and precious. It should be crammed with students drinking in its contents; the lovely, austere eighteenth century English silver and furniture, the hundreds of porcelain groups, each one of which is a little marvel in decoration, the subtle Chinese carvings, the masterpieces of design you will find among the fabrics. I tell you no student could study such things intelligently and remain a bad designer. Far, far better spend the time gazing at those marvels than in stuffy classrooms studying the principles of design.

And with that exhortation I will finish my first article. So far I have dealt only with the more or less general principles of a student's training. In Part Two, I shall deal with the difficulties of making pen drawings and acquiring of a style.

From the sketch book of Arthur Watts.

167

Part Two. January 1935

In Part One, I dealt with the errors that, looking back, I am pretty sure that I made in my general education as an art student, and the methods of training memory and observation that I would use if I could have my time over again. In this, my second article, I am going to concentrate on line drawing.

Well, I remember my chief problem was how to acquire a style. It seems absurd now, because I have gradually learned to use a pen, or brush rather, as you will hear later, in a way which expresses best what I want to convey; and that style, far from being arrived at straight away, is the result of a great deal of experiment and fumbling about. But my style gives me no pleasure in the exercising of it. On the contrary, I am cramped by it, bound by it. I wish to goodness I could break away from it. It has forced me into mannerisms that I constantly repeat. I draw, too often, the same types in the same way. But I have evolved it myself. I have not, knowingly at any rate, cribbed the styles of established artists; and that, just that wholesale cribbing, is an error many

HOW TO SOLVE THE GARAGING PROBLEM.
THE BABY-CAR DAVIT FOR TOP FLAT-DWELLERS OWNING SMALL CARS.

Illustration by E. H. Shepard.

young draftsmen fall into. And what is so tragic is that they copy not what is best in their idol's work, but the worst – perpetrate their most obvious mannerisms, their least satisfactory tricks.

Now, as long as a student is drawing from the life he does not worry about a style. He does not want to imitate the technical achievements of acknowledged masters: he is quite content to put down what he sees as faithfully as possible. In short, he is so anxious to make his drawing like the model, to express and correlate the forms he sees, that he is too busy to worry about questions of technique. And the same applies to the studies he makes in the country and the street. They are, like his life studies, made with charcoal, pencil or chalk, all tractable and easy as no other media are.

THE WOMAN-HATER.

Illustration by H. M. Bateman.

But the moment he gets a pen into his hand, everything is changed. No longer are those first tentative strokes, that can be rubbed out at will, possible. No longer, in fact, can anything be rubbed out. Half tones and broad masses of tone must be dispensed with, and instead an uncompromising metallic point permits of no mistake. Difficult enough to draw anything 'out of your head' with, but when it comes to drawing from the life, or in a figure composition, the very devil of an instrument!

It is just this intense difficulty of his medium, I think, that drives the student to want at first to imitate some acknowledged master of this particular craft with whom he feels himself in sympathy. He looks at the work say, of E. H. Shepard, and observes that the obstacles which to him are insurmountable offer no difficulty to Mr. Shepard at all. Charming girls, no less charming young men, animals, flowers, trees, all flow from a pen that never stumbles. What more natural than that the student should imitate that consummate draftsman? Nothing. Nothing is more natural than to imitate the work of an artist you admire, and nothing is so dangerous.

Illustration by Caran d'Ache.

Look at H. M. Bateman's imitators! H. M. Bateman was obviously influenced by Caran d'Ache. His work still shows that influence. But he has taken only what is best to build his style on, and himself brought a nervous strength and sharpness of line that Caran d'Ache – blessed be his memory – never had. He has not been content to imitate his master's types, but has observed, and created his own. When he wants to express tone, he never uses a meaning-less redundancy of lines, but a wash that gives a pleasant limpidity to his drawing. But he has his faults, such as certain extreme facial exaggera-tions, which his imitators have fastened on to and reproduced ad nauseam; thus harming the man whose work presumably they admire so much, and entirely damning themselves at the same time.

Again, look at the exquisite pen drawings of Edmund J. Sullivan – probably the finest decorative pen draftsman of his time. He, it is equally obvious, was influenced by Albrecht Dürer, and on that great master's genius for expressing form in line he built his own reputation. But, as in H. M. Bateman's case, how intelligently he allowed himself to be influenced, how much of colour and grace he brings himself! And along come his imitators, and once more we find, not what is best in his work, but his easier mannerisms adopted and exploited.

I have mentioned these two artists because they are both essentially stylists, and therefore dangerous in their influence. Shepard is probably less dangerous to imitate, because he has fewer mannerisms, and his skill in handling his pen is so remarkable that it is quite impossible to imitate.

Illustration by Edmund J. Sullivan.

Illustration by Albrecht Dürer.

I always avoided any very slavish copying of one artist: Albrecht Dürer, Caran d'Ache, Claude Shepperson, Adolph Munzer of pre-war *Jugend* (*Jugend* was a pre-first world war avant garde magazine), to name a few of many. I believe if – looking back after all these years – I could accuse myself of directly imitating anybody, it would be George Morrow, whose sad, sedate, middle-aged men are such close relations to my own characters.

Illustration by Claude Shepperson.

Illustration by George Morrow.

Illustration for E. M. Delafield's "Provincial Lady Goes Further"
by Arthur Watts.
Courtesy of Mcmillan & Co. Ltd.

But to go back to this subject of style: I am inclined to think that advice must be negative, must be summed up in this one sentence: "Be influenced, but do not imitate."

In retrospect, I think I should have tried to accustom myself to a pen or brush much earlier. I did attempt, after my fashion, to use a fountain pen instead of a pencil for sketching out of doors, but the flow of ink was always unsatisfactory, and I took to a little stylographic pen, which gave a nasty, scratchy line that never varied. I used to try to draw from the nude with a pen – always with execrable results – and, more often and more happily, in the costume class.

Better, I believe, to have tried at first combining pen and wash, using the pen more as I became more skillful; trying always for simplicity of expression and an economy of line; starting with very simple objects such as a leaf or a flower, and working up through casts placed in a direct light that gave very clearly defined shadows to the human figure. But simplicity, simplicity, that is the goal to strive for, and the most difficult to reach. Not necessarily a startling originality of expression – that is almost as dangerous as a slavish imitation of someone else – but an honesty of expression.

In my next article I hope to deal with the various materials and methods that can be used for line drawings, and a few of the more obvious pitfalls to avoid.

Part Three. February, 1935

In Part Two, I dealt mostly with style, and the pitfalls awaiting those who try to achieve a style too soon. This month I must, to a certain extent, harp on the same theme because, although I want to get on to the various ways of making pen and brush drawings, the construction of these must obviously depend on the style that the artist wishes to adopt.

As I have said before, it is a mistake ever to attempt to dogmatize about any form of art. But one can say, without any fear of contradiction, I think, that the brush is more suitable to a simple and boldly conceived drawing, and the pen better employed on more complicated work. Both brush and pen have their peculiarities.

Let us take the brush first. For flexibility, for the ease with which a fine line can be broadened into a very thick one, it has great advantages over the pen. On the other hand, that very ease, the smoothness with which the brush travels across the paper, is the cause of its greatest drawback: it has a tendency to give a grey line. This is

Pen and brush illustration by Arthur Watts.

the result more particularly when India rubber (eraser) has been used on brush lines. If, on a partially completed drawing, you want to rub out pencil marks, and you rub the inked in part, you will find a marked greying of the line where the rubber has been used. The reason is, of course, that whereas the metallic point of the pen, or nib rather, bites ever so slightly into the surface of the paper, the brush glides over it, and the ink adheres less.

True, the grey will reproduce as black when your drawing is printed, but it is that very fact which can be so disconcerting. Often you will find that a background you put in at the beginning of your drawing, and over which the rubber is frequently used, will look perfectly right in tone in the original, but coarse and hopelessly out of tone in the reproduction. And, unless you realize what has happened, you will probably curse the block maker, although the fault is not his but yours.

The brush is also unsuitable for delicate cross-hatching or rendering masses of lines. Invariably, the part of the drawing so treated, though it may appear delicate enough in the original, will coarsen in the process of reproduction, and the more delicate a line you use the more it will coarsen. This, no doubt, is due to the fact that, for the reasons I have stated above, the brush never gives a truly black line.

Brush illustration by Arthur Watts.

The pen, to anyone that has got in the habit of using a brush, seems harsh and rather capricious. It needs continual cleaning, owing to the density of drawing inks, and should it be dropped, the nib will probably be ruined.

If the paper has a greasy patch, your pen will cease to function at that spot, and you may dip it in the ink over and over again without results. If the surface of the paper is imperfect at any point – as it so often is if you erase carelessly with a razor blade – your pen will splutter.

The pen is most difficult to use over process white. It is not nearly so easy as with the brush to increase the thickness of a stroke, especially on a curve. In short, it is a much less tractable instrument.

Pen and brush illustration by Arthur Watts.

But once you have made a line, you can rub over it as much as you like without it greying to any appreciable extent; and if you want to use masses of fine lines, or if instead of one clear line for an outline you want to use two or three lines very close together, you will find a pen far better than a brush. A decision as to which is the more easy for you to use can be made only after experience and experiment.

Now as to the surface you are going to work on: that again is a matter for constant experimenting, and I advise you to try out every possible kind of paper and board that you can lay your hands on.

I, personally, use nothing but a thick hot-pressed paper. It has not that slipperiness that I find so unpleasant in Bristol Board (though other artists probably find that same slipperiness as pleasant as I find it unpleasant); its surface is not destroyed by erasing with a safety razor blade, and this enables us to avoid using process white, with its loathsome appearance; and it can be easily rolled up for transport.

For a long time I used to make my pencil drawings on ordinary paper, pin a sheet of tracing-paper on top, and make my pen or brush drawing on that. Very excellent this method was for experimenting, because one had the pencil drawing underneath, and could always begin again. But I frequently found, when a particularly elaborate drawing was nearly completed, that I would make some slight error. And that was the devil! You cannot erase with a safety razor blade on tracing paper, or only with intense difficulty; process white, being quite a different tone, looks horrible; and the only way out of the difficulty is to mount the drawing, cut out the bad patch, put another piece of paper in, and produce in the end what is a very blotched-looking affair.

Another drawback is that the pen or brush drawing when mounted looks much coarser than when stretched over the pencil drawing, and owing to the impossibility of getting a pure white tracing-paper, the reproduction looks coarser still. Now that I come to enumerate its disadvantages, I cannot think why I ever used that particular method!

Having collected the various materials together, we come to the actual making of the drawing. And here I find that I pause for a long time. I cannot tell you how to draw with a pen or brush. I cannot tell you how to 'do' trees or people or houses. I can only give you a few general hints, and you must work out your salvation in your own way.

I would say in the first place that a good black and white drawing, besides being well drawn, must have a certain flexibility of line. If the lines are all of the same thickness, the same quality, the drawing will inevitably have a tame anemic appearance. It is the contrasting, and at the same time the blending, of the fine and heavy lines that give it richness.

Pen and brush illustration by Arthur Watts.
By courtesy of the "Radio Times".

I know of no artist – alas that I cannot name a living artist! – whose work holds more of this quality than does that of the late Edmund J. Sullivan. It is even more apparent in his originals than in the reproductions, because he had a habit of using very short detached lines to express modeling. Now one of the rules, the few rules of pen or brush drawing for reproduction, is that a short detached line, or masses of line – or dots – invariably coarsen in reproduction; for this reason, especially when he has represented the faces of women, his work suffers. But there remains brilliancy, a sense of colour that other draftsmen seldom equal.

Second to flexibility, and scarcely less important, is the necessity of avoiding meaningless lines. A line drawing, however complicated in subject, however detailed in execution, should nevertheless give the impression of economy in the means used. Never let two lines do the work of one. If for shadows, or to suggest colour, masses of line superimposed, one over the other at various angles, are used, then those masses should have a pleasant quality of their own. The last thing they should suggest is that the artist has gone on laying one set of lines on another until he has reached the required depth of tone.

Pen illustration by Edmund J. Sullivan for "Herr Diogenes".

And for Heaven's sake don't try to be clever! Much better to be rather dull and tight at first, until you have begun to understand your medium, than to develop too early all sorts of showy tricks from the exploitation of which you will never recover. But these are the only really important rules that can be laid down; for the rest, it is a question of how you want to say *what* you want to say.

Nothing could be less similar than the methods employed by Low and Shepard, for instance, but looking at a figure drawing by either, you will agree, I think, that in their particular style the subject could scarcely have been better said.

Illustration by E. H. Shepard.

Part Four. March, 1935

A very important consideration is how your drawing is going to look when it is reproduced. On the whole I am inclined to think that most students worry too much on that score. A great deal, obviously, depends on the quality of the paper on which the drawing is going to be printed, but for the average papers in use today a few simple rules are enough.

The first is to keep in mind the size that your drawing is going to be when reproduced. However fired by ambition you may be, it is no earthly use producing a complicated drawing measuring two *feet* by three, if all the space your editor or client can give you is two *inches* by three. This is a very common oversight with beginners.

It is impossible to lay down any definite law, of course, because everyone draws in a different way, but I should say that few drawings, however loose and 'sketchy', can stand a greater reduction than to a third of their size, that a half is fairly normal and two thirds about right for rather delicate work. I have seen drawings actually enlarged and looking quite well, but they were invariably very simply drawn.

The second rule, and this applies to any drawing printed on any paper, is that a single fine line, especially a fine, short line, will invariably thicken up in the process of reproduction. I mentioned this pitfall in my last article when I referred to Edmund J. Sullivan; this month I am illustrating its results with one of my own drawings.

This drawing, which appeared in *Punch*, was drawn on 'scraper board' – a board surfaced with china-clay. Its advantage over ordinary papers and boards lies in the fact that it is possible to black over any area, and then work over that area with a metal point. The metal point penetrates the blackened surface, and a white line is made which will reproduce perfectly. It has, as far as my experience goes, only two disadvantages: one, that it is unsuitable for pen work because the surface is so soft; two, when a brush is used the lines tend to become very grey. It is fatal to use India rubber over a completed part of the drawing; in fact it is possible, by rubbing hard, to completely erase a line.

Now if you will look at this drawing you will see that the lines composing the houses on the left are coarse, and give the impression of being stronger than those indicating the traffic; in the original they do not give the impression, but fall back into their proper place. This is because, firstly, they were drawn with a brush, and in the original are not black at all but grey (having had India rubber used

"Progress" by Arthur Watts. (Full page version on page 46.)

over them); secondly, they are composed of single lines and detached masses of short, single lines (the two dangers that I warned you against in my last article!), and thirdly, because the drawing has been printed on unsuitable paper.

But when we get below the windows of the bus the effect is much better; the detail is delicate and true in tone. Look closer, and you will see that much of that detail, the side of the bus and the bonnet of the car following, has been put in with solid black and worked over with a white line. Also the brush work that goes to make the two motor cyclists and their machines has been scored across with white lines. And so faithfully have these white lines come out when reduced that they are almost invisible.

"Coast of Skye" Scraper board drawing by Arthur Watts.

If only I had scored my houses with a fine perpendicular white line they would have receded right into the background as was intended.

The rest of the drawing has come out exactly as it was meant to. You will see what I meant in my last article about flexibility of line when you contrast the heavy brushwork on the tree with the traffic in the street. Some of the foliage is a white line on black, some a black line on white, and the same applies to the tree trunk and the lawn. What delicacy can be got, even on an unsuitable paper, by scoring black lines with white ones will be seen from the door of the house on the right-hand side. But your white line must be used with care or it will look mechanical. Contrast the line work on the waistcoat of the builder's man with that on the statue. The first has just that unpleasant, mechanical quality; it expresses no roundness, no gradation of light and shade, while the second, I believe, does. How I wish this drawing had not left my hands, and I could alter that waistcoat!

One other point about the reproduction of this drawing. If you care to look it up in *Punch* and compare that version with the one in front of you, you will see how important the choice of paper is in the reproduction of line drawings. Obviously a magazine like THE ARTIST, which prints only a very occasional pen drawing, and consists, as I say, almost entirely of half-tone and colour work, has chosen its paper for that purpose, just as *Punch*, which uses practically nothing but pen drawings, has chosen its paper with a very different end in view. Had I been making this drawing I am discussing for THE ARTIST, I should have been more cautious and scored my houses in the background, but that would be the only difference.

It is when one particular drawing has to be used for various grades of paper that the chief difficulties occur. The paper on which such dailies as *The Times*, the *Telegraph* and the *Morning Post* are printed is suitable for quite delicate work, but as likely as not a drawing intended for them will have to be reproduced in all sorts of provincial papers, the surfaces of which are deplorable. Many designers of advertisements are apt to forget this. It is for such work that a white line on black, or a black line scored by white ones, is so invaluable. For a white line will reproduce without thickening on the worst paper, and a black line, if scored by white lines, will tend to thicken far less. An understanding of these two all-important facts will enable a draftsman to produce drawings which, although they will look well on bad paper, will not have that 'commercial' appearance one associates with press drawings.

There are various tricks that can be used for line drawings. The mechanical tint and spatter work are the two best known. A mechanical tint is employed to give a tone over any particular area without having recourse to masses of line. All that is necessary is to indicate with blue lines the patch or area that you want so treated, and the process engraver will do the rest. If you are fastidious, you can get a sheet of specimen tints from any block makers showing the strength and patterns that can be obtained. Each has a number, which you can indicate on your drawing, and you will then know exactly the strength of tone that will be used.

Splatter work is another and rather less mechanical way of getting tone, and is produced by covering up the drawing with a mask of paper and cutting out the area to be treated. You then splatter ink with a toothbrush on that area, and a more or less pleasing tone results. It is unreliable on poor paper.

Part Five. April, 1935

Illustration by George Belcher.

In my last article I dealt with the various methods that can be employed in making black and white drawings. It has occurred to me since how little there really is to be said on the subject. Apart from those two all-important factors – the quality of the paper on which the drawings are to appear and the size that they will be when reproduced – everything depends on the personality of the artist. If he is good at his job, if he has something to say that he feels himself, if he is drawing primarily *because* he has something he wants to say and only secondarily because he wants to get a living, he will inevitably build up for himself a style that is suited to his personality.

In this article I am dealing with humorous – which is the refined word for comic – art. It may be – I dare say it is – a lowly branch of art, but it is absorbing, and one in which it is difficult to excel. The comic artist is generally represented by the press as a rather dissolute fellow dashing off to some *jeux d'esprit* in the intervals of drinking bouts. But – for I count myself as one of that rather unhappy band of brothers – we're not like that really. We are rather a serious folk with a kind of mental astigmatism that compels us to draw life – although we draw life as we see it – a little crooked. And, all said and done, do we draw life so very crooked? As crooked, say, as do fashionable portrait painters and magazine illustrators? Are George Belcher's charwomen any less true to life than the simpering debutantes one sees at the Royal Academy? Or are George Morrow's mild, spectacled businessmen any less convincing than the eagle-eyed Mayors and Aldermen seen in the same institution? I doubt it. In any case, a desire to represent, to interpret character, to comment good – or bad – humouredly on the life around him, in short, to be fascinated by the human scene, is the one absolutely essential quality to be possessed by the comic artist above all artists. He must represent what he sees and not what other draftsmen who have gone before him have seen, or his work, even if technically flawless, will be valueless.

176

Illustration by Rowlandson.

Art must be the result of observation, of selection and rejection of material, in a word it must be based on life. And this seems to be particularly true of comic art. All the great comic draftsmen – Rowlandson, Cruikshank, Doyle, Leech and the rest – have each of them produced not merely a type but scores of types that we recognize as living people, and in that fact lies their greatness. Opposed to them are draftsmen of no mean accomplishments, such as Baxter, who invented Ally Sloper and filled a paper week after week with the adventures of that once famous personage and his friends. But nobody wants to look at Ally Sloper now, nor could anyone laugh at him if he did. And that, I think, is because, though scarcely more vulgar and certainly no more revolting than Rowlandson's drunken bucks and blowzy women of the town, Ally Sloper and his like have not, and never really had, any relation to living people. They were characters invented entirely in their creator's brain, and do not really

Illustration by Cruikshank.

convince. But in studying Rowlandson's swarming crowds one knows that one is looking at eighteenth century life – distorted by the artist's vision, it is true, but none the less vivid for that. So that, if you are going to be a good comic draftsman, it is not enough to refrain from cribbing other draftsman's types. It is not enough even to invent your own types; they must be related to life – life, or some aspect of it rather, given a twist by your own personality.

Illustration by John Leech.

Another point about comic art is the importance of being able to set your characters in the scene to which they belong. The more convincingly you render their surroundings – the more convincingly you can render your characters in their surroundings – the more convincing your drawing will be. If your situation takes place on the deck of a ship, then draw the deck of a ship, and don't just suggest a bit of a ventilator and a little planking. I do not say that there are not first-rate comic drawings produced without surroundings; there are. But if you try to extend your humour to the accessories as well as the principal figures, you will have a far wider scope.

Look at the drawings of the three men I have mentioned before, Rowlandson, Leech and Cruikshank – three of the greatest comic draftsmen England has produced – and see how harmoniously the characters move in their surroundings. Then turn to Phil May, who rarely bothered himself with a background. And see if his drawings do not look a little thin by comparison. No, my young friends who want to be comic draftsmen, don't run away with the idea that, by drawing a man in a hat too big or too small for him, by handing on traditional jokes about tramps being offered uneatable puddings by young wives, you are ever going to be anything but hack draftsmen. You will want as much sense of design, as much sense of character, as any serious artist and, in addition, you will want the essential quality of viewing

Illustration by Phil May.

any situation with a fresh eye. You will need to be continually making studies from the model, in the street, of any object that might be useful in your work, or you will soon fall into the snare of so many comic draftsmen, that of repeating continually the same type, the same situation.

The drawing which illustrates this article I have chosen because it is a good example of what I mean about figures fitting into their surroundings. True, their surroundings are themselves, but that makes the problem not less, but more, difficult. This picture is essentially a scene. You will notice, too, how useful a mixture of brush and pen has been; the brush for the actual figures in the foreground, the pen for the finer lines in the reflections. And, if the drawing has no other value, it is at least an effort to render a difficult subject truthfully, without balking any of its problems.

"There's nothing like you in the world Ethel" by Arthur Watts.
(Full page version on page 95.)

Part Six. May, 1935

Now that I have come to the last of these articles on black and white drawing, I find myself wondering how much I have said that is of any practical use to a student. And I have gone over them in my mind and come to the conclusion that, whether what I have written is of any use or not, I've said all I have to say.

It is so very difficult to lay down hard and fast rules about drawing; one man's meat is so very much another man's poison that, with the exception of those few tips, shall I say, which I have given you, I can only theorize – approach the problems from my own particular point of view. You must fumble around and find your own salvation. But what may have some interest, I think, if it is not any actual help, is a short *précis* of my own beginnings and strivings to arrive at some sort of career.

Well, I come from those army circles where an artist is still looked at with more than suspicion. My father did not know any artists and certainly did not want to. Only by the most resolute idleness at school, where for my last two years I occupied the bottom place in the lowest form on the engineering side, did I finally convince him that I might as well spend my time in an art school as anywhere else.

But even at school I had made my bow to the public. My first employers were a firm who owned a great many papers of the *Snap Shots* type, and amongst these was a paper called the *Boy's Champion*. For the *Boy's Champion* – which long ago died – I used to draw diagrams of those tricks with corks and pins and bottles with which little boys love to bore their relations. I received one and sixpence for each drawing. And as my technique improved so did the quality of my commissions, and I remember I did the seven wonders of the world (culled from early Victorian engravings) at half a crown each.

I cannot remember if these successes in the world of art impressed my father, but about this time he gave way to my ambitions and I was sent to the Goldsmiths' Institute Art School. There, except for a certain amount of drawing from the life, I thoroughly wasted about two years. There was then, and probably still is, an institution known as the National Competition. Students sent in work once a year and were awarded a gold, silver or bronze medal. These medals were so many feathers in the caps of the schools to which they were awarded, because the more medals the higher the grant allowed to the school by the Board of Education.

The consequence was that, instead of studying, students were encouraged to produce highly finished and meretricious works in the hope of winning medals. I remember I executed a lot of book illustrations myself, which won a silver medal. They were figure drawings done 'out of my head' as they say. I made no studies for them because I had not learnt and was not taught to use a model for figure drawings.

I had all this time only the haziest idea of what I wanted to do, which in itself was a great drawback. I suffered then, as I have suffered all my life, from a diffidence that prevented me from aiming high. Oddly enough, I had no wish at all to make comic drawings. If I did want to do anything, it was decorative book illustration such as Edmund J. Sullivan excelled at.

I left the Goldsmiths' Institute under a cloud – I seem to remember unpleasantness over locking a master into a room – and bobbed up at Slade School. Here, from my point of view, I was even worse off than at the Goldsmiths', except that I worked hard at drawing from the life. In those days the Slade authorities frowned at anything but

Title page for "The Horoscope" by Arthur Watts

the fine arts, and drawings for book illustrations and the press were summed up as "the sort of thing you see in the *Graphic*". I used also to attend the Regent Street Polytechnic for lessons in book illustration, but I am afraid I used that excellent institution rather as a club than an art school.

From the Slade I drifted to Antwerp where, because we were locked in during working hours, I worked even harder at the life, and then on to Paris where I learnt little about drawing and a lot about living. And so once more back to the Slade.

Still, at twenty-one, I had no idea how I was to make a living until one day I made a drawing of something that struck me as funny and sent it to *London Opinion* which, under Lincoln Springfield, was then in its heyday. I forgot about the drawing until I received a cheque, together with a letter from the art editor to the effect that further contributions would be acceptable. I had found my real métier. Encouraged by the fairly frequent appearance of my work in that very bright little paper I haunted the offices of such magazines as the *Strand*, *Pearson's* and the *London*, and they gave me from time to time articles and stories to illustrate. *The Tatler* used my drawings occasionally and Comyns Beaumont encouraged me in the *Bystander*.

Oddly enough, that infernal diffidence of mine to which I have previously referred stopped me from ever sending a drawing to *Punch*, and it was not until 1912 when I happened to meet Lawrence Bradbury and was given an introduction by him to F. H. Townsend, the then art editor, that I made my first contribution to that paper.

It was about this time (1912) that I took to drawing from a bird's-eye view, and because so many people regard it as a freakish eccentricity it may be worth while explaining the reason for it. I always tried to induce editors to give me a page to myself, my argument being that if a drawing was worth using at all it was worth a whole page. But I found that in an upright shape the figures

Arthur G. Watts

bulked too large and there was no room for the background. And as my style of humour leaned towards subjects in which very often the background was as important in developing the idea as the figures, I had to think of some way of getting round that difficulty. And the bird's-eye view was the obvious solution. And that is all!

Well, just as I was beginning to make a pretty tolerable living, war came and for four years I could get a drawing done only at rare intervals, so that in 1919 I had practically to start again. But in 1920 I was fortunate enough to get in touch with a firm of artist's agents who were of invaluable assistance to me.

And here let me digress for a moment on the subject of artists' agents. For an absolute beginner, with all his way to make, they are not, I think, of very much use. It is for him to make some sort of connection; when he has got his name a little known, in however narrow a field, they can then widen that field for him and almost certainly increase his prices. But they should be chosen with the greatest care. In my own case, I was, as I say, extremely fortunate and I soon found a wide range of work open to me that I should not have found for myself.

I persisted right up to about 1927 in attempting to become a serious artist. I had then the ambition to illustrate expensive books such as Arthur Rackham and Edmund Dulac made fashionable. I got my chance at last, and the book was an abject failure. Since then I have abandoned all pretence to be taken seriously and executed, to the best of my ability, whatever came my way.

I continually make studies, I continually make experiments, and I live in a state of profound discontent with what I produce. I know that even in the last ten years my work has improved beyond all knowledge, but what I can do doesn't give me much pleasure and what I can't do gives me considerable pain – and that seems to me the proper state of mind for any artist.

'Commercial work' I consider a cant phrase. Any art is commercial in that the artist is willing to trade it for bread and boots and the amenities of life, and there is no reason why a drawing made to advertise a tobacco should not be as good as a picture

Illustration by Arthur Rackham.

Arthur G. Watts

made to hang on a wall. But I think that artists whose work is to be used in connection with the press or advertising should regard their clients as honorable enemies and try with all their might to inflict on them what they, rather than their employers, want. For, believe me, if you are going to let your clients get the upper hand, if you are going to be content to be a tame artist turning out hack work, you would do far better to abandon drawing as a profession altogether.

Don't think I mean that at the beginning of your career you are to be truculent and uncompromising; that will get you nowhere. But try to produce work a little better that what is asked for; try by degrees to get your own way – that is half the fun.

arthur watts

The Last Drawing

This was the last of Arthur's drawings for *Punch* and one
of his finest. In the late 1940s, my sister, Marjorie-Ann and
I raced this same boat, called 'Summer Haze', in the Padstow
regattas. In 2002, when the original boat was nearly 100 years
old, I measured her and began building an exact replica on
Middle Island, Nova Scotia, Canada. The new boat
named 'The Silver Thread' will be launched in 2004.

Simon Watts

"Aye, my father was drowned, and my father's father, and <u>his</u> father 'afore him."

arthur watts

Stolen Artwork

As this book was being prepared, the following original pieces of artwork were stolen from the editor's San Francisco apartment. At time of publication, they had not yet been recovered. If you have any information on the whereabouts of the pieces listed, Simon Watts would be most appreciative if you would inform him at **info@arthurwatts.com** or contact Algrove Publishing Ltd. by telephone, fax or letter. The stolen pieces are:

Page 16 - Force of Habit

Page 42 - "Mind where you're going, Ethel..."

Page 89 - Courtesy Then and Now

Page 91 - "Is Mrs. Jones there..."

Page 95 - "There's no one like you..."

Page 150 - A Modern Christmas

Page 160 (also cover illustration) - "Flown the Atlantic..."

Algrove Publishing Ltd.
36 Mill Street
Almonte, Ontario
Canada K0A 1A0
Telephone: (613) 256-0350
Fax: (613) 256-0360